TOUCHING
THE HEM

Jesus and the Prayer Shawl

TOUCHING THE HEM

Jesus and the Prayer Shawl

By John D. Garr, Ph.D.

GOLDEN KEY PRESS
Restoration Foundation
P. O. Box 421218
Atlanta, Georgia 30342, U.S.A.

*To my colleagues
around the world who
have enshrouded Pat
and me with loving
concern and have
covered us in the mantle
of their prayers.*

TABLE OF CONTENTS

Introduction

The four Gospels that introduce the Christian Scriptures are of inestimable importance to every Christian believer in the world. Their reports of events in the life of Jesus and their record of the divine words which he uttered form the very basis of Christian faith.

The writings of the entire New Testament Scriptures, however, contain many statements that are virtually impossible to understand if they are taken out of their original context and interpreted in the light of modern cultures. In order to understand what is written, we must faithfully employ the grammatico-historical method of scriptural interpretation which enables us to interpret Scripture within the context of the grammar and the historical and social setting in which it was written, cutting the straight line of interpretation that constitutes "rightly dividing the word of truth."[1]

The lives that Jesus and the apostles lived and the words that they spoke were manifest in the context of their contemporary Jewish culture and of their religion, Second Temple Judaism.[2] The language they spoke was in all probability Hebrew (or at least Western Aramaic, a sister lan-

guage of Hebrew).[3] Virtually everything they said
and wrote was first thought in Hebrew (or Aramaic) and then translated into Greek. If we are to
understand the written record of their teachings
and of the events of their lives, we must, therefore, study both the *Koinè* Greek of the Apostolic
Writings and the Hebrew language and Semitic
thought that underlie the Greek text. We must
also have a thorough knowledge of the history,
culture, and traditions of the first century Jewish
people, including their political milieu, their socio-
economic circumstances, and their religious practices.

Frequently, very important–even essential–el-
ements necessary for an accurate understanding
of what is recorded concerning Jesus' life and ministry are obscured by inadequate translation and/
or interpretation of the text itself. We must use as
a point of initiation for any New Testament interpretation the fact that Jesus was an observant
Jew and that everything he said and did was di-
rected toward his Jewish contemporaries. He himself declared, "I am not sent but unto the lost sheep
of the house of Israel."[4] The God whom he addressed as Father was YHWH, the God of Israel;
the Bible that he used was the *Tanakh*,[5] the Hebrew Scriptures; the soil which he traversed was
Israel, the land of the Jews;[6] and the people who
were his family, friends, associates, and even his
detractors were Jews. In order to understand the
record, therefore, we must look at it through Jewish eyes, or at least we must discard our Greco-
Roman and Euro-American eyeglasses and don
Hebrew lenses.

When we engage ourselves in a search of the Apostolic Writings[7] to discover what the authors said—and not what our presuppositions want them to say—we find a gold mine of enriching truth that transforms our lives into the image of God's dear Son. Every event reported by the evangelists in the Gospels takes on new meaning, because we see the living Jesus not as some extraterrestrial cosmic Christ but as the Son of man, the Jewish Jesus living out among his Jewish brethren the paradigm of what it is to be fully human. When we see what the essence of God was when he made himself flesh and tabernacled among us, we understand much more about his absolute deity. We discover that Jesus truly put a face on the Father[8] by manifesting himself as the "radiance of God's glory and the exact representation of his being."[9]

A knowledge of the Hebrew foundations of Christian faith is vital for all believers in Jesus as Messiah and Lord. By understanding the ancient system of praise, worship, and service through which Jesus and the apostles expressed their devotion to God, we comprehend the motivations for their actions and the basis for their teachings. Christian faith acquires a new depth and meaning when it is understood in the light of the Hebrew matrix from which it emerged. Faith in Jesus is then elevated and expanded, given new depth and meaning, not diminished or subsumed into Judaism. The living Messiah is truly seen to be the one who elevated the faith of his heavenly Father and of his fathers according to the flesh by fulfilling it,[10] reforming it,[11] and restoring it to its inherent ideal.[12]

This book explores just one event in the life of Jesus that has for two millennia inspired millions of people with faith in God. It is but one example of the profound wealth of knowledge and inspiration that is often hidden just beneath the surface of Bible translations which do not convey the details or original import of what is reported in Scripture. There are multiplied thousands of other scriptural events and concepts that yet remain to be explored as we continue to dig into the inexhaustible resources of the infinite Word.

I am deeply indebted to some of my closest colleagues and friends for insights that have formed either the basis or the spark of insight upon which many of the ideas outlined and detailed in this book are based. Among them are Dr. Karl D. Coke, president of Redirection Ministries, for his insightful teaching and his writings that have appeared in "Prayer Lessons from Jewish Culture" in *Restore!* magazine and in syllabi for The Timothy Program International; Dr. Douglas A. Wheeler, president of Mended Wings, for his provocative and challenging article, "The Law of the Fringe," that was also published in *Restore!* magazine; Dwight A. Pryor, president of the Center for Judaic-Christian Studies, for his informative audio teaching, "The Mystery of Jesus' Prayer Shawl"; David Bivin, editor of the *Jerusalem Perspective* for his pioneering exposition, "The Hem of His Garment," that appeared in that journal; and Dr. Charles Bryant-Abraham for his masterful theological and linguistic suggestions and help with the manuscript; and to Judy Grehan and

Sandy Clark for their careful and constructive reading of the manuscript.

I believe that as you read these pages you will be challenged to draw nearer to the living Jesus, to walk humbly with him in faith, and to come to the full knowledge of the Son of God.[13] This is the immediate and lasting benefit of understanding the Jewish roots of our Christian faith: we find a foundation of historical and theological truth that anchors our confidence in God's completed work in Christ and sets us on the road to walking with him in maturity and completeness. Understanding the Hebrew foundations of Christian faith is, indeed, a golden key that unlocks the treasures of Holy Scripture.

It is my hope that as you share in this wealth of understanding you will be challenged to "search the Scriptures" to discover for yourself these and untold numbers of additional golden nuggets of truth that will enrich your life. We recognize both the Hebrew Scriptures and the Apostolic Writings as the "God-breathed" Word of God[14] when we fully realize that they are inexhaustible and that the mercies and truths of God which are contained therein are "new every morning."[15]

John D. Garr, Ph.D.
Passover, 2001

---

[1] 2 Timothy 2:15. The Greek word for "rightly dividing" is ὀρθοτομέω (*orthotomeo*) which means to "cut a straight line."

[2] By the first century of the common era "Biblical Judaism" had undergone development that began with Ezra and the "Men of the Great Assembly" and continued through the Tannaim, including the schools of Hillel and Shammai. In many ways, Jesus and the apostles sought to reform Second Temple Judaism by restoring it to biblical foundations, perhaps even encouraging a return to biblical Judaism.

[3] Historically, conventional scholarship has agreed that Western Aramaic was the predominant language of Judaea at the time of Jesus; however, some more recent scholars have suggested that since personal and business documents found at Qumran among the Dead Sea Scrolls were written in Hebrew, Mishnaic Hebrew could still have been commonly understood and spoken in Judaea. Since Jesus and the apostles were focused on religious issues, they could well have taken the tradition of synagogal liturgical use of Hebrew (translated contemporaneously into other languages) as their guide, thinking and teaching in Hebrew. This would explain the insistence of certain of the Apostolic Fathers that Matthew's Gospel was first written in Hebrew.

[4] Matthew 15:24b.

[5] The word *Tanakh* is actually *TaNaKh*, an acronym for *Torah* (the Pentateuch), *Nevi'im* (Prophets), and *Ketuvim* (Writings–historical and poetic books). Jesus himself made use of this Jewish tradition of the three divisions of the Hebrew Scriptures (e.g., Luke 24:44).

[6] Jesus did venture into Samaria (John 4:4-9) and Phoenicia (Matthew 15:21).

[7] The term *Apostolic Writings* describes what is most commonly termed *The New Testament*. In reality, the New Testament is not a book, but a covenant introduced by Jesus in fulfillment of Jeremiah 31:33. The books of Matthew through Revelation comprise a record by the apostles (or others under their auspices) of the events that occurred under the New Testament.

[8] John 1:18; 14:9.

[9] Hebrews 1:3, NIV.

[10] Matthew 5:17-19.

[11] Hebrews 9:10.

[12] Matthew 5:21-48.

[13] Ephesians 4:12-13.

[14] 2 Timothy 3:16-17.

[15] Lamentations 3:23.

Chapter 1

A Healing Touch

"If can just touch his garment, I'll be healed!" This statement is the centerpiece of one of the most poignant of all Bible stories, an event that unfolds in what was probably a very ordinary day in the life of Yeshua of Nazareth. The humble, unassuming Galilean peasant had long been sought out by increasing numbers of suffering people who desperately needed relief from a virtually unending list of maladies and misfortunes. His compassion for the poor, the infirm, the mentally retarded, the emotionally unstable, and the economically and politically disenfranchised had become legendary. He reached out with an empathy that few had ever seen, and he changed lives with a healing touch that had never before been observed.

This lowly Nazarene had been born some thirty years earlier under most inauspicious circumstances. While a few enlightened believers understood Jesus to be a virgin's son, none of those among whom he grew up ever saw anything extraordinary, much less supernatural, about him.[1] Much of the general public, and certainly his detractors, considered him illegitimate, born in a stable, wrapped in swaddling clothes.

In keeping with the strong devotion to their Jewish faith, his parents had circumcised him on the eighth day, thereby initiating him into the covenant of Abraham. They had presented him at the temple[2] where the astonishing words of both prophet and prophetess predicted wonderful things for his life that would have far-reaching and profound consequences for Israel and the world.[3] He was reared inconspicuously by his family in a town west of the Sea of Galilee whose only claim to fame was that no good thing had ever come from Nazareth.[4]

Jesus had been precocious, to be sure, debating at the age of twelve with Israel's greatest teachers during his family's pilgrimage festival observance. But, for the most part, his life was that of an ordinary Jew. Taught in home, synagogue, and temple in Judaism's great truths, he "grew in wisdom and stature, and in favor with God and men."[5] He was employed in his father's business, that of a builder, soiling his hands and straining his body in the construction industry of his day. When he reached the age of thirty, he set out on an itinerant teaching ministry, announcing the imminent breaking forth of the kingdom of God.[6]

Immediately, those around Jesus recognized him to be a rabbi; this, despite the fact that it is nowhere recorded that he had been a student either of Beth Hillel or Beth Shammai, the era's two leading schools of rabbinic thought. He was unique as a teacher, however, for his hearers attested to the fact that he spoke with an authority that the other teachers of his time did not manifest.[7] He was a lover of the land of Israel and of the common folk. His teaching championed honesty, integrity, and human dignity.

Jesus also possessed an amazing gift for the supernatural. Though other Hebrew holy men of that time had frequently manifested supernatural powers, when Jesus spoke, he did so with unheard-of authority so that people were healed *en masse*, demons were exorcized, even the dead were raised. Because of this, some began to think that perhaps he was Elijah returned in spirit and power to prepare the way for the Messiah. Others considered that he might be Jeremiah or another of the prophets.[8] Since there had been no recognized prophet in Israel for some four centuries, this was a distinct honor in itself.

Then, one day as he inquired of his disciples who they considered him to be, Peter, the most outspoken of his followers, exclaimed, "You are he, the Messiah, Son of the living God."[9] Jesus reiterated the fact that there was nothing about his person that would have identified him as such: it was a revelation of the Eternal Father. Though he had consistently referred to himself as "Son of Man," both a term of humility (connoting merely a "human being") and a Messianic title, and despite the fact that he had ascribed to himself eternal preexistence in his "I AM" statements,[10] Jesus' identity as the divinely Anointed of the Jewish people and the Savior of the world had been largely hidden from both the public and his disciples.

On this day, therefore, as he went his way, teaching and touching the lives of those who came to him, one of those who had heard of his reputation for compassion and of his power to mend broken, diseased bodies and wounded, troubled souls was a woman with a life-threatening condition. We cannot be certain about the details of this story, but we can imagine, based on what is recorded, that her condition was grave. Frail, emaciated, anemic, she was but a shell of her former vivacious, ebullient self. Her youthful beauty had dissolved into the haggard look of weakness. Her ashen face was punctuated by the thin lips and the clenched jaw of a determination to survive. She was desperate. "If I can just touch the hem of his garment, I'll be healed," she said to herself.

This poor woman had been hemorrhaging for twelve years, probably with menorrhea, a condition that rendered her both physically weak and psychologically depressed because her malady made her perpetually unclean according to the ceremonial laws of her people and had probably long since been cause for divorce as "unfit for cohabitation." If she even touched other people, they contracted ritual impurity, and they would continue to communicate her "uncleanness" to others unless they immersed in a ritual bath and waited until evening to be pronounced "clean" again. How embarrassing! In such desperation, these words of hope echoed like a chant, rising like a crescendo in her troubled mind: "If can just touch his garment, I'll be healed!"

Trying to find a cure for her condition, she had spent all of her resources on physicians and had only grown worse, perhaps even the victim of medical malpractice or ineptitude. Now, here she was, a poverty-stricken, emotionally wrecked, physically broken waif, possessing only one faint hope of deliverance from certain death: "If can just touch his garment, I'll be healed!" she repeated to herself.

So, defying all social convention, she mustered up the last reserves of her strength and pressed her way through the multitude that was thronging the Rabbi, hanging on his every word, and reacting to his every gesture. How she made her way through the crowd, no one knows, but in her heart of hearts she just knew, "If can just touch his garment, I'll be healed!" She didn't need a word; she needed a touch. And, touch him she did. In one desperate lunge, she reached out her bony, near-lifeless hand and brushed against just the hem of Jesus' garment. The fact that she touched just the hem of his garment may be an indication that she was crawling through the thronged, huddled bodies. A miracle happened: immediately her hemorrhaging stopped. She was completely healed!

Jesus realized that something had occurred because of the release of power from his own person. When he inquired, "Who touched me?", his disciples replied incredulously, "With this multitude thronging you, how can you ask, 'Who touched me?'" Then she who had been stooped, emaciated, and cowering suddenly stood tall, so tall that she could not hide herself in the crowd, and she confessed to the Rabbi what she had done. Even though he might have been rendered ceremonially unclean by the biblical society's standards, Jesus affirmed this woman's hopes, saying, "Daughter, thy faith hath made thee whole; go in peace, and be whole of thy plague."

What a wonderful story of extraordinary and powerful emotion! Desperation and faith produced a profound miracle for a simple daughter of Israel. What a wonderful Savior, this Jesus, who had the power to heal just by being touched even when he was unaware of what had happened! "If can just touch his garment, I'll be healed!"–words that have echoed through the anals of history, inspiring faith and hope in the hearts of millions of believers in the Jesus of the Gospels.

But, there's more to the story!

[1] See Matthew 13:54-57 and Mark 6:1-3.

[2] Luke 2:22-24.

[3] Luke 2:32.

[4] John 1:46.

[5] Luke 2:52, NIV.

[6] Matthew 11:12, the centerpiece of Jesus' proclamation concerning the kingdom should be translated: "The kingdom of God is breaking forth [*like the walls of a sheepfold*], and passionate men press their way into it."

[7] Mark 1:22.

[8] In Second Temple Judaism, the concept of *gilgul ha-nephasot* was a common view, suggesting that the spirit of one prophet could return upon someone else in another era. This concept is alluded to in Luke 1:17 in Gabriel's annunciation to Zacharias and in Matthew 11:14 in Jesus' evaluation of John the Baptizer. This phenomenon is likely interpreted as being the return of the spirit (or the frame of mind or line of thought) that motivated a man of God of one era upon another person in another time. It may well also have implied that God could return that measure of his Holy Spirit which distinctively motivated a prophet in one era upon another person at a subsequent time.

[9] Matthew 16:16 (author's translation).

[10] John 8:58; 11:25; 14:6.

Chapter 2

The Hem of the Garment

If the story in Matthew 9 were just an isolated, one-of-a-kind event in the life of Jesus, we might think that this woman was merely acting out of humility (just wanting to touch the extremity of the Rabbi's garment) or desperation (touching only what she could reach). In Matthew 14:35, 36, however, this story is reported: "And when the men of [Gennesaret] had knowledge of him, they sent out into all that country round about, and brought unto him all that were diseased; and besought him that they might only touch the hem of his garment: and as many as touched were made perfectly whole."

Could it be that touching the hem of Jesus' garment became a common practice, with untold numbers of people–not just one woman or the diseased of one region–healed by such a simple touch? Why were so many people fascinated with and inspired by the "hem of his garment"? Why was this part of Jesus' clothing so important that it became a point of contact for the expression of faith that brought deliverance to all who touched it?

Hidden from the eye of the reader of these

stories is an enriching key to understanding what
actually occurred on these days of deliverance.
Virtually all translations of these passages of Holy
Scripture render an incomplete portrayal of the
actual object of the desperate woman's determined
hand and of the touch of the diseased of
Gennesaret. Most Christians imagine Jesus wearing a sumptuous robe and the woman touching
the broad richly embroidered band that was the
hem of his robe. After all, as one person was heard
to remark, "That's the way Jesus looked in all the
photos we have of him!"

Most versions of the Bible tell us that she
touched the "hem of his garment"[1] or the "border
of his garment"[2] or the "edge of his cloak"[3] or the
"fringe of his cloak."[4] None of these translations,
however, adequately conveys one important detail of the event. Without this detail, we simply
miss the richness of this event and of an entire
tradition in biblical history.

The word in the Greek text for "hem" is
kraspedon, which literally means "the fringe of a
garment; the appendage hanging down from the
edge of the mantle or cloak, made of twisted wool;
a tassel or tuft." *Kraspedon* is the Greek word that
was used to translate the Hebrew word *tzitzit* in
the Septuagint Greek Version of the Hebrew Scriptures. What the woman touched, then, was not a
broad decorative band at the bottom of Jesus' garment, but the fringe, the twisted woolen tassel
hanging from the edge of his mantle or cloak.

This more accurate depiction of details of
Jesus' garment helps us understand more about
his life here on earth. Jesus was in every way a

very proper Jewish man. He was a Bible-believing, observant Jew who had been trained by his parents in doing "everything according to the law of the Lord,"[5]   This Jesus was a Jew, and the religion which he observed throughout his lifetime was the faith of his fathers. He made no bones about it: "We know what we worship: for salvation is from the Jews," he declared.[6]

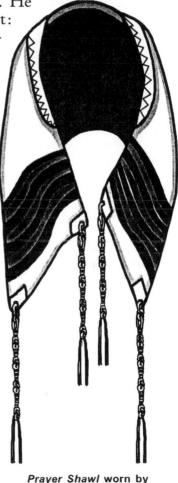

Jesus was recognized as being Jewish by the woman at the well of Samaria by the clothing that he wore. His grooming and his style of dress immediately identified him as a Jew. The outer garment that he wore was called in Greek *himation* or in Latin *pallium*, meaning a rectangular, four-cornered cloak, mantle, or tunic. This differed from the Roman *toga*, which was semicircular in design. In Hebrew, this garment was first termed *adderet* or *me'il*. Later it came to be called *tallit*. Some have suggested that the Hebrew word *tallit* is an adaptation of the Greek *stole*,[7] from

Prayer Shawl worn by Jewish men

which we get the name of the vestment that is still worn today by liturgists in sacramental churches.

We can be certain that Jesus observed the Jewish traditions for grooming and dress because they were requirements of the Torah (law), the violation of which was sin (cf. 1 John 3:4: ". . . sin is the transgression of the law."). Because Jesus was born "under the law,"[8] sinlessness for him meant complete Torah observance, including the commandments governing dress and grooming. Since the record of Scripture emphatically affirms the fact that Jesus was without sin,[9] we must draw the conclusion that he was fully observant of the written law of God in its most minute detail. His contentions with his fellow Jews over legalisms and hypocrisy, including those denunciations of "broad" phylacteries and "long" fringes, were focused entirely on interpretations of Torah and applications of oral tradition, not on the authority of the Hebrew Scriptures, the written Word of God. Jesus, himself, testified: ". . .I have kept my Father's commandments."[10] He was a Torah-observant Jew; therefore, he was not negligent in obeying his Father's commandments regarding dress and grooming.

When the woman and the people of Genessaret touched the *tzitzit* on Jesus' *tallit*, they were fulfilling a Hebraic tradition of respect for God and his Word. What they did was not profoundly unusual in first century Israelite society. For the common people, their sages were living examples of separation unto God's Word; therefore, their clothing and other items associated with them had special significance, even sacredness. It was an honor to touch a rabbi's clothing. Being healed by the touch of a prophet, sage, or miracle worker also occurred not infrequently in Israel.

Jesus the Jew, then, was merely continuing the tradition of many before and during his time, of reaching out to the oppressed with a hand of mercy. The woman and the citizens of Gennesaret were operating in that same tradition when they reached out to grasp the *tzitzit* that Rabbi Jesus wore. They were laying hold on the visible symbol of the totality of the Torah and by doing so were touching in a spiritual dimension the God of the universe.

Originally, the word *tallit* (pl. *tallitot*) meant "gown" or "cloak" and referred to the rectangular, four-cornered, blanket-like mantle worn by men in ancient times (quite similar to the *poncho* of Latin American culture). It was made either of wool or of linen[11] and probably resembled an *'abbayah* ("blanket"), the oriental robe still worn by the Bedouin Arabs for protection against the weather.[12] A *tallit* of finer quality resembling the Roman *pallium* was worn by the wealthy and by distinguished rabbis.[13]

This may have been the *tallit* that was also described by the Hebrew word *sadiyn* (Greek: *sindon*), a rectangular piece of fine linen worn as an outer garment during the day or as the sole garment at night. These were the fine linen garments that the woman of valor was praised by her husband for making. This passage in Proverbs 31 is said to have originated in Abraham's praise for Sarah and as such may be an indication of an even more ancient origin for the *tallit* or at least of its precursor, the *sadiyn*.

This expensive fine linen garment was also used to cover the bodies of the dead. This may well further throw light on the fact that during his entombment, Jesus was wrapped in fine linen. He was likely covered by Joseph of Arimathea with a fine linen *sadiyn* or *tallit*, so that both in life and in death, Jesus was physically covered with the outward symbol of the authority of God's Word, the Torah.

Initially, the *tallit* was not an extra vestment (as in later times). It was merely the outer four-cornered garment to which the *tzitziot* were appended.[14] According to Jewish tradition this garment had to be a hand's breadth shorter in length than the garment under it.[15] The inner garment was a tunic (called *haluk* in Hebrew) and could be worn in the home or when one was engaged in physical activity where the outer robe would be too cumbersome. The outer garment, the *tallit* (*himation, pallium*), was essential for public occasions, for despite the fact that the inner robe extended to just above the ankles, it would have been considered immodest in Jewish society for one to appear in public without the *tallit*. If necessary, one could appear in public only in a *tallit*, but not solely in a *haluk*.[16] Recognizing the fact that two robes were worn in Jesus' time helps us to understand his statement in Matthew 5:40 (NIV): "If someone wants to sue you and take your tunic [*haluk*, tunic], let him have thy cloak [*tallit, himation, pallium*] as well." It was better in Jesus' mind for one to appear immodest than to be a contentious person.[17]

After the dispersion of the Jews in the Babylonian captivity, the Jewish people adopted the fashions of their Gentile neighbors. This was particularly true of the majority of the captives who chose to remain outside Israel following the exile. Such conformity to popular styles of dress was not unusual, however, for the Jews had always assimilated garment designs from their neighbors, simply adapting *tzitzit* to the fashions of the day.

As time progressed, many of the Jewish people found themselves wearing clothing that had no distinctive corners to which they could attach fringes; therefore, the traditional *tallit* gradually faded into disuse. Anxious to maintain fulfillment of the commandment, however, the Jews decided to retain the robe, not as a main garment, but as a shawl or surplice worn as a religious garment: the prayer shawl. The name *tallit* was maintained through the centuries for this liturgical garment. By wearing this surplice during the day, the Jewish people could continue to wear the *tzitzit* (fringes), which were essential to the fulfillment of the commandment.

Again, as fashion changed and the wearing of a fringed surplice became an oddity, the Jewish people began to wear the *tallit* only for prayer, in both home and synagogue.[18] Until well after the destruction of the Temple and the Roman occupation, the Jews in Israel continued to wear the *tallit* as a simple outer garment with *tzitziyot* attached in the four corners. The transition from *tallit* and *tzitzit* that were worn throughout the day to *tallit* as a praying shawl was not complete for Jews until centuries later. The modern "prayer shawl" dates only to the time of Medieval Europe.

Obviously, this was not the original intent of the *mitzvah*, for the *tzitzit* was to remind the Jews of the commandments at all times, requiring that they be worn at all times. At an early period, the answer for many Jews was to devise a "*tallit katan*," a miniature *tallit* complete with fringes that could be worn under the outer garments. This garment, also called "*arba kanfot*" (four corners), is a rectangular piece of cloth made of linen, silk, or wool with a hole in the center through which the head can pass. It has the four essential corners to which the *tzitziyot* are attached. Orthodox men wear the *tallit katan* from the age of three throughout their lives.[19] This is in keeping with Rashi's observation that "it is more important to be garbed in *tzitzit* in the hours other than the time of prayer in order that one remember at all times, and not go astray and commit a sin; for at the time of prayer one does not sin."[20] Even in death, a Jewish man is wrapped in his *tallit* with one of the *tzitziyot* cut or removed (which renders it invalid).

Rudolph Brasch made this observation concerning the historical transition of the *tallit* among the Jews: "A positive symbol of a life dedicated to God fell in stature to the role of a praying-shawl. The tsitsit, once proudly and visibly worn as a signpost to pure living, were relegated to form part of an undergarment, often deteriorating in people's minds from an ethical symbol to a superstitious talisman. Yet, in spite of such temporal devaluation and displacement, the tallit itself always preserved its potent symbolism . . . No deterioration could detract from its mission. Today, when the Jew puts on his tallit, numerous thoughtful and incisive messages stir and challenge his mind."[21]

It has been suggested that the Jewish people could avoid the entire commandment of tzitzit by simply not wearing a garment with four corners, for the tzitzit is required to be appended only to the corners of such a garment. As styles of clothing changed over the centuries, Jews could perhaps have discontinued this practice altogether; however, the commandments regarding the wearing of fringes required the Jews to make for themselves fringes "throughout their generations," which implied that even in generations when Israelites no longer were accustomed to wearing four-cornered garments, they should still make four-cornered garments and attach tzitziyot to them, thereby fulfilling the Numbers 15:38 commandment "throughout the generations to come" (NIV).

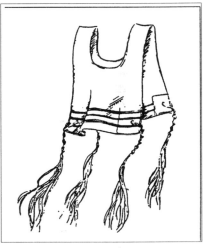

Tallit Katan worn by many Jewish men

Due to the gradual change in the style and manner of fulfilling the commandment of tzitzit, we cannot know the exact state of the tallit in

Jesus day with absolute certainty. We can be sure, however, that it was not the prayer shawl of modern times. Misunderstanding this historical fact has given rise to one edition of the *New International Version's* translation of Matthew 23:5: "They make . . . the tassels of their prayer shawls long [*kraspedon . . . hima-tion*]." In the days of Jesus, the *tallit* had not yet become the modern praying surplice, used at the time of morning prayer. It was still an outer garment worn throughout the day when one was in public. Incidentally, it is quite ironic that, while this edition of the *New International Version* translates the Greek words *kraspedon . . . himation* as "tassels of their prayer shawls" when referring to Jews and hypocrisy in Matthew 23:5, it translates precisely the same phrase (*kraspedon . . . himation*) as "edge of his cloak" when referring to Jesus and divine healing in Matthew 9:20.

What we do know for certain is that since Jesus was a faithful, Torah-observant Jew, he fulfilled God's commandment to wrap himself in the *tzitzit* which was the forerunner of the modern prayer shawl. To the general public both from Israel and from the nations round about, he was immediately recognized as a Jew by the flowing tassels that were attached to his mantle. He, too, like all observant Jewish males of his day, was a walking reminder that God's people were to remember all his commandments and do them.

[1] Matthew 9:20.
[2] Luke 8:44.
[3] Matthew 9:20, NIV.
[4] Matthew 9:20, NRV.
[5] Luke 2:39.

[6] John 4:22.

[7] W.O.E. Oesterly. *The Religion and Worship of the Synagogue* (London: Pitman & Sons, 1911), p. 451.

[8] Galatians 4:4.

[9] 2 Corinthians 5:21; 1 Peter 2:22.

[10] John 15:10.

[11] Talmud, *Seder Kodoshim, Mas. Menachoth* 39b.

[12] Alfred J. Kolatch. *The Jewish Book of Why* (Middle Village, N.Y.: Jonathan David Publishers, 1981), p. 100.

[13] Talmud, *Seder Nezakin, Mas. Baba Bathra* 98a.

[14] If a garment did not have four corners, it was exempted from the *mitzvah* to add *tzitzit*.

[15] Talmud, *Seder Nezakin, Mas. Baba Bathra* 57b.

[16] David Bivin. "The Hem of His Garment." *Jerusalem Perspective* (Issue 7, Apr., 1988), pp. 4-5.

[17] David Bivin. pp. 4-5.

[18] Rudolph Brasch. *The Judaic Heritage: Its Teachings, Philosophy, and Symbols* (New York: Van Rees Press, 1969), p. 236-238.

[19] Alan Unterman. *Jews: Their Religious Beliefs & Practices* (Boston: Routledge & Kegan Paul, Ltd., 1981), p. 140.

[20] *Zohar*, III:226.

[21] Rudolph Brasch, *The Judaic Heritage: Its Teachings, Philosophy, and Symbolism*, p. 239.

Chapter 3

A Mark of Remembrance

From the giving of the law at Sinai, the *tallit* had certain identifying characteristics that set the Jewish people apart as being chosen of God. What made it uniquely characteristic of the Jews was the fact that God required his chosen people to append one *tzitzit* (tassel) in each of the four corners of their outer garments. This is the commandment of the Torah: "Speak unto the children of Israel, and bid them that they make them fringes in the borders of their garments throughout their generations, and that they put upon the fringe of the borders [corners] a ribband of blue: and it shall be unto you for a fringe, that ye may look upon it, and remember all the commandments of the Lord, and do them; and that ye seek not after your own heart and your own eyes, after which ye use to go a whoring: that ye may remember, and do all my commandments, and be holy unto your God."[1]

This commandment is reiterated in Deuteronomy in a more concise form and without added explanation: "Make tassels on the four corners of the cloak you wear."[2] The implication of these statements is that when one looked upon

the *tzitzit* he would remember God's commandments and seek after God's heart, not his own
ways.

Most Christian theologians in history have
faulted the Jewish people for their literalist interpretation of these and other passages, disparaging
their faithfulness to do exactly what God had commanded them as "legalism" or an attempt to be
justified before God "by works," rather than "by
faith."

The truth is that each of the practices that
God enjoined upon the Jewish people was in per-
fect keeping with his continuing use of symbols
and markings to single out and set apart times,
places, and various material articles as semaphores
directing his people's attention to his Word and
commandments. God is a marking, identifying
God. He establishes memorials to awaken in the
hearts of his people memories of his great acts of
deliverance and to generate faith for his continuing intervention in their behalf. Remembering
God's mighty acts and his ongoing faithfulness to
his covenants and his people is a manifestation of
faith, not of legalism, of dependence upon God's
loving-kindness (*chesed*), not upon human actions
as means of acceptance before God. Remembrance
is central to worship both in Judaism and Christianity. Indeed, both faiths are centered in and
function as calls to remembrance.

Due to the fact that men are finite and live
within the constraints of time, they tend to forget
things in the past. If markers are not placed to
ensure remembrance, past events tend to be forgotten, particularly from generation to generation.

Everyone laughs about tying a string around a finger so something will not be forgotten, but, in essence, God has done just that for his people at various times and in various places, creating markers in time, geography, and dress, both to single out his people as unique bearers of his name and to call to their remembrance his mighty acts on their behalf and his ongoing covenant with them.

More eloquent than words, a simple symbol speaks more powerfully than speech. This is why body language is more revealing than spoken words. As one walks through life, with all its pitfalls and diversions, symbols that demand his attention and restore the memory of his divine calling and its requirements are invaluable. Christianity is filled with these symbols: crosses, banners, vestments, stained-glass windows, and the currently ubiquitous "WWJD" ("What Would Jesus Do?") emblems (which someone has called "Christian *tzitzit*"!). For the Jew, the *tzitzit* of the *tallit* are silent, yet powerful symbols that point his heart to God.

Yitzhak Buxbaum described symbols this way: "If we deepen our devotion to God, and cultivate the habit, many, many things will remind us of Him. For example, when you see an animal with horns, you will be reminded of the *shofar* (the ram's horn) and of the High Holidays and all they signify; or when you see a body of water, you will be reminded of how God split the Red Sea for our ancestors. This is a slight touch of love-madness for God. As in the words of [Maimonides], in our love for God we should be like someone 'who is love-sick, and cannot take his mind off the woman he loves.' "[3]

The concept of marking, singling out, or identifying is characteristic of God in another way.
He places marks on his people to signify their
separation or sanctification unto himself. His chosen people are not to be like the other peoples of
the earth. While they are not to cloister themselves in a ghettoized existence isolated from the
rest of the world, they are to be distinct both in
their conduct and in their appearance. This is why
God told Abraham, "Leave your country, your
people, and your father's household, and go to
the land I will show you."[4] This is the reason for
his instruction to Moses: "You must not worship
the Lord your God in [the heathen's] way."[5] It
was for this reason that Jesus also implored the
Father concerning his disciples: "My prayer is not
that you take them out of the world but that you
protect them from the evil one."[6] This concept of
being in the world but not of the world has characterized God's Chosen People from time imme-
morial. Often it has made them a "gazingstock"
for the secular and pagan societies in which they
have lived.

Because their unique lifestyle and appearance
have differed from societal norms, the Jewish
people have been targeted by those bureaucrats
who have always vented their frustration against
anything that did not conform to societal norms
with massive campaigns of persecution and vio-
lence. Persian Prime Minister Haman, the arche-
type for anti-Semitism, declared to his king: "There
is a certain people . . . whose customs are different
from those of all other people . . . it is not in the

king's best interests to tolerate them."[7]

God established parameters to limit his people's conduct and appearance both to keep them separate and to bear witness through the marks in their lifestyle and their persons to the fact that they were his chosen people, a testimony that he alone is God. The *tzitzit* tradition was one manifestation of God's spirit of marking that singled the Jewish people out as uniquely his and bore a public witness to the nations and peoples round about them that they were a God-dedicated people. The *tallit* was, in effect, a uniform that identified them as God's army, a force for peace and justice in the earth.

Through the ministry of Jesus, this uniform became the Holy Spirit himself, which clothed the believer "with power from on high," so that they could be witnesses to the living, incarnate Torah to "the ends of the earth."[8] The transition was from external material marking to internal spiritual marking, from an external uniform to a spiritual garment, the Holy Spirit. The effect, however, remained the same. God's people of all ages are to be singled out by markings that identify them in the world as his Chosen and serve as constant reminders that they are to fulfill his commandments and do his will. The *tallit* was such a mark of remembrance.

Following God's commandments and the leading of his Spirit involves complete submission to the divine will, a total dependence upon God. The fringes that God required his people to attach to their garments reminded them not only of his commandments but also that they were not to live their lives after their own ways. Theirs were to be lives not only of obedience but also of trust, not only of submission but also of living faith.

In the wrappings, twistings, and knottings of the *tzitzit* is found the mystery of this principle. In Psalm 25:1-3, King David declared, "O my God, I trust in thee . . . let none that wait on thee be ashamed . . ." In Isaiah 40:31, the prophet declares that those who "wait upon the Lord shall renew their strength. . ." The word translated "wait" in these passages is *qavah*, which literally means "to twist, to bind as in a rope." It is also the normal verb "to hope," the root of which is seen in the Israeli National Anthem, *HaTikvah* (The Hope). Those who want to be successful in their relationship with God, mounting up with wings as eagles, will find themselves making a spiritual *tzitzit* daily by twisting, tying, and binding their lives together with the life of the Lord, thereby gaining the strength that is needed for victorious living. The Holy Spirit, indeed, is the *shamash*, the longest, helper strand of the *tzitzit* that binds the believers' lives together with the life of God. And, those who have wisdom will see that they are tightly wrapped in relationship with the God of the universe.[9]

The mantle (*tallit*) was not in itself unique to Israel. What was unique was the fact that it was to have "fringes" in its "borders." The Hebrew word for "fringe" is *tzitzit*, which also means tassel or lock. The word for "border" is *kanaph*, which primarily means wing, but also can be translated as corner or edge. This corresponds to the Greek description of Jesus' garment recorded in Mark 6:56: ". . . they . . . besought him that they might touch if it were but the border [*kraspedon*] of his garment."

The *tzitzit* is also called *gedil*, meaning intertwined threads or twisted work (cf. Greek: *kraspedon*, "twisted wool"). The *tzitzit* features a tassel of threads that are wrapped and knotted. Some have suggested that the knots were originally designed to indicate the binding of evil spirits as the *leitmotif* of tying and loosing knots was seen to parallel binding and loosing demons.[10] The written Torah, however, is not specific regarding the construction of *tzitzit*. Various traditions have specified different ways in which the threads are to be wrapped and knotted. The Karaites, who are not recognized as part of the Jewish community because of their fundamental biblicism and rejection of the "Oral Torah" tradition, knot the threads and literally make the *tzitzit* each time it is worn. When they are not wearing the *tzitzit*, it

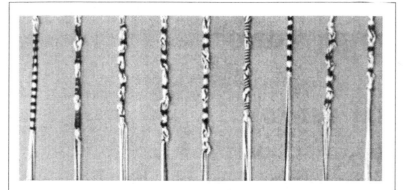

Some of the different traditions of tying *Tzitzit* *(P'Til Tekhelet Photo)*

is hung in a prominent place in the home so that they may literally "look upon them" and be reminded of the *mitzvot*.

The Torah was very specific about the number and placement of the *tzitziyot* in the outer garment and about the purpose of their being so displayed. Deuteronomy 22:12 declares, "Make tassels on the four corners of the cloak you wear." There were to be four *tzitziyot*, with one set in each of the four corners of the cloak (*kesuth*). The purpose for their placement was equally clear: ". . . that ye may look upon it, and remember all the commandments of the LORD, and do them."

Until this time, clothing for mankind had served only as a reminder of the sin of Adam and Eve when they rebelled against the one commandment which God had enjoined upon them. Indeed, the Hebrew word for garment (usually the outer garment or *tallit*) is *beged*, which is derived from the verb root *bagad* meaning to rebel or to be faithless. Perhaps God had allowed the garment that he gave to cover man's nakedness to serve as a continuing reminder of his rebellion. Now, God took the symbol of sin and death and made it a reminder that he had set before Israel a choice between life and death, between blessing and cursing. The opportunity for life was found in faith toward God and obedience of his commandments that were vividly impressed upon their memories by the *tzitziyot* that were now to be appended to the four corners of their garments.

Metaphorically, the four corners of the *tallit* call to mind the four corners of the earth and the four directions, underscoring the fact that "the earth *is* the Lord's, and the fulness thereof; the world, and they that dwell therein" and that "all the earth shall be filled with the glory of the Lord."[11] In whichever of the four directions the Jewish man turns, the *tzitzit* in that corner of his *tallit* makes him conscious of the omnipresent Creator and Lord of the universe.[12]

Rebbe Reb Zusya, of Hanipol, offered this suggestion for remembrance of the way of God: ". . .as soon as you wake up in the morning, take in your hand the holy *tzitzit* [many men wear their *tallit katan* while sleeping] and direct your mind and heart to meditate on the greatness and majesty of the Creator, blessed be He, and take on yourself the true fear of God—to have awe and fear because of His greatness. This should not be just a matter of rote and habit."[13]

There has never been a regulation in Judaism as to the size or length of the *tzitziyot*. Some five decades before Jesus' time, "The elders of the School of Shammai and the School of Hillel . . . reached the decision that there is no prescribed length for the tzitzit."[14] This, of course, led to some ostentatious displays by those whose devotion to God's Word knew no bounds and by those who wanted to appear more powerful and/or holy to the public than they actually were. One Jerusalem resident was remembered as being so devout that he was nicknamed, "*Ben Tsitsit HaKeset*," because of his "long tassels that literally trailed behind him on the ground."[15] Though this man may well have been devout, there were others who merely made a hypocritical display that was condemned by Jesus in Matthew 23:5: "But all their works they do for to be seen of men: they make broad their phylacteries, and enlarge the borders [*tzitziyot*] of their garments." Though there were those who were thus deplored not only by Jesus but also by their fellow Pharisees, the vast majority of Jewish men in Jesus' day and in every generation before and after that time wore the *tallit* with *tzitziyot* with a pure heart, reminding them that they were to fulfill the commandments of the Eternal and not walk in their own ways.

Jewish men throughout history have been like the man described in the Talmud who did not yield to the temptation to commit an immoral act when he noticed the *tzitziyot* on his garment and was thus reminded that he would have to account to his Creator for the sin he contemplated.[16] The *tzitzit* has fulfilled God's design by summoning its wearer to recall the commandments of their God and to do them. For the vast majority of Jewish men in history they have been exactly what the Eternal designed them to be: constant visual reminders that their wearers were covenanted with God to remember all of his commandments and to observe them.

The Jewish people were to be a peculiar treasure unto God, a kingdom of priests who should love God with all their hearts, souls, and strength[17] and should manifest that love by fulfilling all of his commandments (*mitzvot*). Jesus was operating in complete accord with his own Jewish heritage when he made this same observation to his disciples: "If you love me, keep my commandments."[18]

A loving God designed a system of reminders to assist his chosen people in remembering his commandments and expressing their love to him: he provided visible markings in their clothing and elsewhere that constantly summoned them to obedience to his Word. This practice was a privilege, a badge of honor through which one could visibly demonstrate his commitment to the Word of God.

[1] Numbers 15:38-40.
[2] Deuteronomy 22:12.
[3] Yitzhak Buxbaum. *Jewish Spiritual Practices* (Northvale, N.J.: Jason Aronson, Inc., 1990), p. 34.
[4] Genesis 12:1, NIV.
[5] Deuteronomy 12:4, NIV.
[6] John 17:15, NIV.
[7] Esther 3:8, NIV.
[8] Luke 24:49; Acts 1:8, NIV.
[9] This concept is amply illustrated in Karl D. Coke's audio teaching, "The Prayer Shawl," and in Doug Wheeler's "The Law of the Fringe," *Restore!* (Vol. 3, No. 2), pp. 28-32.
[10] W.O.E. Oesterly, p. 452.
[11] Psalm 24:1; Numbers 14:21.
[12] *Zohar*, III:175b.
[13] Rebbe Reb Zusya, quoted in Yitzhak Buxbaum, p. 84.
[14] *Sifre* Numbers 11:5 to 15:38, quoted in David Bivin, p. 5.
[15] David Bivin, p. 4. See Samuel Safrai, *The Jewish People in the First Century*, p. 798, note 3.
[16] Talmud, *Menachoth* 44a.
[17] Deuteronomy 6:5.
[18] John 14:15.

Chapter 4

A Prayer Closet

The use of the *tallit* to separate oneself totally to communion with God was an institution in Judaism before the time of Jesus. This is perhaps the extended meaning of Jesus' recommendation concerning prayer in Matthew 6:6: ". . .when thou prayest, enter into thy closet, and when thou hast shut thy door, pray to thy Father which is in secret. . ." The Greek word for closet is *tameion*, which means "an inner chamber, or a secret room." The closeting of oneself in the covering of the *tallit* was a symbolic separation from the world around the Jewish man. While the more ostentatious Pharisees made a show of their alms giving and their public prayers, the greater percentage of the Pharisees were sincere in their separating and secreting themselves in prayer so that with *kavanah* (proper attitude and concentration) they approached God and entered into a knowing relationship with him. While men in Jesus' time never covered their heads when praying as many modern Jews do, they did wrap themselves in their *tallit*, separating themselves unto God.

Prayer is not the chanting of a mantra in some mindless exercise that seeks to elevate one's consciousness and place him in contact with the "god within." It is not the "vain repetition"[1] *ad nauseum* of words and phrases, be they ever so lofty or inspiring. It is not reading, with mind detached, the words of a prayer book. It is not genuflection or self-flagellation. It is not the loud, public boastings of relationship with the Divine. Prayer is an intense, intimate, personal interaction between God and man. It is a dialogue in which one speaks to God and hears from God. It is a conversation that occurs only when man is intensely focused entirely on communion with God, having shut out all outside influences and distractions.

Rabbi Simeon in the *Mishnah's* tractate *Pirke Avot* 2:18 affirmed this truth: ". . . be scrupulous in reading the Shema and in prayer. When thou prayest, make not thy prayer a fixed form, but make it an entreaty and supplication of love before the Almighty. For the prophet Joel has said, 'Gracious and compassionate is he, long-suffering and abundant in mercy, and repenting of evil.'"[2]

When the Jew wraps himself in his praying mantle he excludes everything external so that his soul is consumed in thought about and in reverence toward God. He realizes that just as the *tallit* envelops his person, so his faith, to be effective, must involve the totality of his life. For him, therefore, there can be no dichotomy between the secular and the spiritual. Everything from the mundane to the sublime–the totality of life–is spiritual. Either God is manifest in every arena of life, or he is not manifest at all.

This is the kind of prayer life Jesus enjoined upon his disciples. Prayer, said the Master, is not a public display of vain repetitions, characterized by verbosity. Prayer is communication with God, and it is best manifest when one is focused on it by any means that can separate one from outside distractions. The Jewish man's *tallit* encloses him in a secret chamber, a prayer closet, shutting out the mundane, elevating his spirit into a knowing relationship with God.

It should also be noted that the prayer which Jesus instructed his disciples to pray was but a condensed version of various prayers employed in the synagogues of that day. It emphasized their relationship with God as Father, a long-standing tradition in Jewish worship, where God was addressed as "*Avinu, Malkeinu*" ("Our Father, Our King"). It honored the holiness and sovereignty of the one God. It asked, as all Jews do daily, for the emergence of the kingdom of God and for the manifestation of God's will in earth just as it is fulfilled in heaven. It petitioned God for necessary sustenance (so that one would not forsake God by being rich, nor dishonor God and himself by being placed in the position of having to steal bread[3]). It sought forgiveness of sins in the tradition of the Jews by first forgiving wrongs brought upon oneself by others. Then, it concluded with the petition for divine guidance, not into temptation, but into deliverance from evil. All of these affirmations and petitions were firmly rooted in the Jewish tradition of the *Tanakh* (Torah, Prophets, and Writings of the Hebrew Scriptures) and of the sages of Israel.

When one prays the prayers of God's Word in a condition of complete trust and concentration, he closets himself in the presence of God. For the Jews, this condition has been best reached by being covered with the praying mantle, the *tallit*. Since medieval times, some Jews have extended this practice to include the covering of the body, as well as the head, in complete separation unto God.

Whatever means one must use, he is constantly invited to the "secret place of the Most High" to enter into communion with the Almighty in an experience that transcends a mere logical, mental exercise and brings one into an encounter with the Divine in which he can worship with all his heart, soul, mind, and strength.

[1] Matthew 6:7.
[2] Quoted in David deSola Pool. *Book of Prayers, According to the Custom of the Spanish and Portuguese Jews*, Second Edition (New York: Union of Sephardic Congregations, 1992), p. 241.
[3] Proverbs 30:8-9.

Chapter 10

A Blessing Covering

It is a tradition in Judaism that blessings be performed under the *tallit*. The benedictions are Torah blessings; therefore, the *tallit* is a reminder that the power of God's Word blesses his people. Notable among these events are the blessing of children and the wedding ceremony.

When younger children receive the blessing of Jacob and the Aaronic benediction[1] they often stand under the *tallit*.[2] It is traditional after the *Shabbat* meal for the Jewish father to bless his children with the words of God recorded in Genesis 48:20, Numbers 6:24-26, and Isaiah 11:2. The father places his right hand on the head of each of his children and prays the following blessing: "May God make you like Ephraim and Manasseh [for sons] Rachel and Leah [for daughters]. The Lord bless you and keep you; the Lord make his face shine upon you and be gracious to you; the Lord turn his face toward you and give you peace. So they will put my name on the Israelites, and I will bless them. [At this point, the father may add a personalized blessing for his son or daughter.] May the Spirit of the Lord rest upon you–the Spirit of wisdom and understanding, the Spirit of coun-

Jewish children being blessed
under the *tallit*

sel and of power, the Spirit of knowledge and of the fear of the Lord–and may you delight in the fear of the Lord." Performing this blessing under the *tallit* reinforces for children the theme that God protects his people through the commandments of the Torah and through his provisions to bless the descendants of Israel always. A blessing is, in effect, a covering, an enshrouding of the one blessed in the providence of God. What better way to demonstrate this truth for children than by pronouncing God's blessing upon them under the covering of the *tallit*.

When a Jewish wedding takes place, the ceremony is generally performed under a *chuppah* (canopy), which is often a *tallit* held aloft by four men, especially in the Sephardic tradition.[3] (The Ashkenazi tradition often uses an embroidered cloth stretched over four wooden poles and set up under the open sky, preferably in a synagogue courtyard.) It is considered essential that this most important rite of passage in Jewish life be covered by the symbol of the Torah and of God's protection. The *chuppah* (canopy) of the *tallit* "represents the future home of the newly married roofed with sanctity."[4] Since the Torah is the source of the commandments that a man is to be joined to his wife and that husband and wife are to be fruitful and multiply, it is only proper that the one most visible symbol for the commandments of the Torah should be employed in the wedding itself. As a canopy it covers the bride and groom with the symbol of God's authority and of obedience to his commandments. It also symbolizes the divine protection of health and happiness of those who abide under the shadow of the Torah's marriage institution. Again, this is not just a mere talisman or amulet. It is a visible symbol of the very words of God.

Perhaps the precedent for wedding under the *chuppah* of a *tallit* was set at Sinai when Israel was espoused in marriage to God. The record declares that the holy mountain was enshrouded in clouds and smoke from the presence of the Almighty. Israel had been summoned from Egypt by the voice of God to appear before his mountain and receive the covenant of marriage that joined them in relationship with their God. And, indeed, the cloud and fire of his presence had accompanied them from the time of their exodus from Rameses until they came to Sinai. This covering with clouds as a symbol of divine protection can easily be seen in the expectation of God's covering presence both in marriage and in the blessing of children that he has ordained in his word.

This principle may also be seen in divorce, that painful process which sunders marriage. Divorce can be described as a rending of the covering garment of blessing upon a sanctified (or set apart) union. It may well be seen as a severing of the *tzitzit* of the *chupah's tallit*, removing the blessing of God's Torah upon the marriage and rendering it *pasul* or invalid. Just as ripping a *tzitzit* from one's *tallit* in biblical times represented a severing of authority, so a marriage is voided, its blessing severed through divorce. Because God hates divorce,[5] this is the reason for Jesus' injunction that man should not separate what God has joined together under his blessing.[6]

Both in the symbolism of blessing upon the constitution of marriage as being covered by the *tallit* and in the rending of the blessed state in divorce, one can see the importance of protecting and maintaining the covering of blessing, the enshrouding of God's provision for health and well-being in marriage. Whatever is done in blessing through the provision of God's Word is an overshadowing of the wings of the Almighty, the covering of the Divine Presence that brings health and security.

[1] Genesis 48:20; Numbers 6:24-26.
[2] Efraim M. Rosenzweig. *We Jews* (New York: Hawthorn Books, Inc., 1977), p. 60.
[3] Alan Unterman, p. 151.
[4] W.O.E. Oesterly, p. 314.
[5] Malachi 2:16.
[6] Matthew 19:6, NIV.

Chapter 5

An Ensign for a Prayer Nation

Considering the predominance of secularists both in the Zionist movement and in the earliest stages of the restoration of a Jewish homeland, the design for the Israeli flag that has represented the State of Israel for more than fifty years is nothing less than extraordinary, perhaps evidence of divine providence.

There can be no doubt but that the hand of God was at work in divine sovereignty, orchestrating the circumstances which led to the United Nations' recognition of the statehood of Israel in 1948. The prediction that Isaiah had made over twenty-five hundred years before was literally fulfilled when the nation was "born in a day"![1]

Amos had predicted that the time would come when the Jewish people would be planted in their own land, "never to be plucked out again."[2] It would have seemed to any logical thinker, however, that such a thing would be an impossibility. No people in history had been conquered and scattered across the face of the globe only to return and restore their national sovereignty after nearly two millennia. Indeed, most Jews had reconciled themselves to the reality that such a restoration could come only in the Messianic Age and had resigned themselves to make the best of their situation by assimilating into the political processes of the nations in which they had been dispersed.

Then, at the end of the nineteenth century, spontaneously and with little realistic expectations, the Zionist movement was birthed. Men of unusual passion arose to insist that both the nation of Israel and the Hebrew language were to be restored so that the Jewish people could have a measure of self-determination and security. Theodor Herzl championed the cause before governing authorities in the western nations. The recognition that the movement received with the Balfour Declaration only twenty years later was amazing.

In the 1930's anti-Semitism reared its ugly head in Germany in the form of the Nazi party and its leader, the megalomaniacal Adolph Hitler, who found an easy scapegoat for German economic conditions in its Jewish population. As Europe was plunged into World War II by the expansionist attacks of the German blitzkrieg, Hitler and his henchmen escalated their overt anti-Semitism, proposing a "final solution" to the "Jewish problem," nothing less than a mass-extermination of Jewish men, women, and children.

Thus began the *Holocaust*. Systematically and unrelentingly, Jews were rounded up throughout Europe wherever the Third Reich rose to power. At first, they were executed and buried in mass graves. Later, a more efficient killing system was devised. Jews were herded into railroad cattle cars and transported to specially prepared death camps. They were brought into gas chambers that were disguised as showers, and lethal cyanide gas was introduced, killing all the occupants. Then, after their corpses had been desecrated, removing anything of value, including in some cases even their skin, they were reduced to ashes in the crematoria. In the end, the *Holocaust* claimed the lives of over six million Jews, including more than one million children.

When the war concluded and the Allied forces discovered the full nature of history's most grotesque and concentrated atrocity against any people group, the corporate conscience of the world was pricked by the plight of the Jews. Part of this guilt resulted from the fact that the Allied nations shared complicity in the slaughter of the Jews by not allowing early Jewish immigration into their nations and then by not intervening when they had gained knowledge of the concentration camps and the systematic slaughter that was being carried out there.

Finally, the United Nations recognized the Jewish people's right to self-determination in establishing their own state in the land of their ancestors. On May 14, 1948, the leaders of the new Israel declared its official constitution. Thus was the nation of Israel restored after nearly two millennia of nonexistence. Its formation and recognition by the United Nations was a miracle; however, its survival in its earliest years was a greater miracle as Israeli patriots defended the tiny infant nation despite being vastly outnumbered by hostile surrounding nations.

In October of 1948, the Provisional Council of the State of Israel adopted the blue and white colors with the Shield of David as the flag of Israel. This flag was unfurled on May 11, 1949, at Lake Success in New York when Israel became the fifty-ninth member of the United Nations. It has flown over the nation for more than fifty years now, a testimony to the sovereignty and faithfulness of God in bringing to pass his prophetic promises to his chosen people.

The design of the Israeli flag is the same as that of the Zionist flag that was used at the First Zionist Congress in Basel, Switzerland, in 1897. David Wolfsohn, the distinguished Zionist leader who succeeded Theodor Herzl as president of the World Zionist Organization in 1905, was instrumental in working out this design. Here is Wolfsohn's own account of the development of the Zionist flag which became the Israeli flag:

> At the behest of our leader Herzl, I came to Basle to make preparations for the Zionist congress, to assure its success and to avoid any opening for detractors. Among the many problems that occupied me then was one which contained something of the essence of the Jewish problem: What flag would we hang in the Congress Hall? . . . Then an idea struck me. We have a flag—and it is blue and white. The *tallit* (prayer-shawl) which we wrap ourselves when we pray: that is our symbol. Let us take this *tallit* from its bag and unroll it before the eyes of Israel and the eyes of all nations. So I ordered a blue and white flag with the Shield of David painted upon it. That is how our national flag, that flew over Congress Hall, came into being. And no one expressed any surprise or asked whence it came, or how.[3]

Amazing? Yes! Apropos? To be sure! It doubtless was a stroke of divine providence that the nation which God originally chose to be a kingdom of priests should, in its restoration, be represented by a flag patterned after one of observant Judaism's clearest symbols of subjection to divine guidance and protection, the *tallit*. God predicted that the temple of his people would be a "house of prayer for all people." Israel is to be a praying nation. It is altogether appropriate, then, that the symbol of this nation should be patterned after the prayer shawl in which observant Jews wrap themselves for morning prayers.

Perhaps divine providence gained ascendancy over secularist, agnostic Jews who established the initially socialist government in Israel. The flag that has flown over the state of Israel for more than fifty years has been a symbol of prayer, even though many officials have been neither Torah observant nor devoted to prayer. Just as the individual Jew covers himself in the *tallit* as a symbol of his being enshrouded in the Torah and thereby in God, himself, so the nation, whether wittingly or not, is covered with the same symbol of blessing and divine protection.

The Israeli flag may well even be a material reflection of the spiritual statement which King David made to Israel: "Thou hast given a banner to them that fear thee, that it may be displayed because of the truth."[4] Being patterned after the *tallit*, it certainly is designed after an object which represents and displays truth (the Torah) to Jews around the world. It also represents God's sovereign action in ensuring that the banner that is unfurled over the restored nation of Israel should demonstrate his intentions to overshadow his people with his wings, using his Torah as a guardian for them until the advent of the Messianic Age.

---

[1] Isaiah 66:8, NIV.

[2] Amos 9:11-15.

[3] Quoted in "The Flag of Israel," a brochure produced and distributed by the Information Department of the Embassy of Israel in Washington, D.C.

[4] Psalm 60:4.

Chapter 6

Sharing a
Rich Tradition

The wearing of *tzitziyot* or tassels attached to the four corners of the outer garment (whether the ancient mantle or the more modern prayer shawl) is a rich tradition of devotion to the specific details of a divine commandment. Jews of every generation who have sought to fulfill this commandment have done so because of the divine initiative some four millennia ago which brought our father Abraham into relationship with El Shaddai and because of God's summons of their ancestors to Sinai to enter into covenantal relationship with him. One must remember that this practice is the result of divine imperative, not man's invention: it was God's commandment to his people, not their scheme to secure or maintain his attention.

The *tallit* is a memory device of divine design that for centuries has served the function of demanding each descendant of the Sinai *kahal* or congregation (*kehillah* in modern Hebrew) to "remember all of the commandments of the Lord and do them."

For those who know nothing of the biblical basis for the *tallit* and *tzitzit* and for the Jewish literalist interpretation of the commandment and tradition which surrounds its continuing use, the practice may seem quaint and anachronistic. Indeed, many modern Jews regard the *tallit* tradition in this manner. For those who make it a part of their daily devotion to God and his Word, however, it is rich in meaning.

Some have suggested that the *tallit* represents nothing more than a talisman, a superstitious effort to contact the Divine. Theodor Reik has proposed that the *tallit* is really a woolen surplice intended to complement the leather *tefillin* as a "quasi-shamanistic attempt on the part of the Jew to dress up like his ancient totem animal."[1] The reference is to the statues of the golden calf that were erected by Aaron at Sinai and by Jeroboam at the Beth El sanctuary. We must remember, however, that both of these instances occurred in times of rebellion against the true worship of God and were judged as such with profound consequences. Though many of the Israelites frequently involved themselves in the pagan rituals employed in worship of the tribal deities of their neighbors, there is no evidence that Israel wor-

—Jewish Father and Son
in their *Tallitot*

shipped God through totemistic symbols of a sacred beast.[2] Reik's suggestion would be correct if he had simply noted that the Jewish people's wrapping themselves in *tallit* both in ancient times and today has been an act of *imitatio Dei*, for this act of remembrance of all the commandments of the Eternal is the ultimate act of submission to the divine will expressed in the Torah and represents an effort to be like God. Just as God shelters all who believe on him under the wings of his divine protection, so the Jews are covered by the winged corners of the garment that manifests Torah to them.

For the Jew in life and in death, the *tallit* is a symbol of the equality of man. A Chassidic saying has it that "when two Jews associate on an equal footing and discuss a subject of Torah, the indwelling presence of God is with them. But when one of them holds himself superior to the other, God is not there."[3] Judaism was the first grand experiment in the democratization of religion. To the Jew, every human being is a "child of God," born equal, distinguished only by virtue. This is why all Jews "conceal the superficiality and diversity of their everyday clothing, covering them[selves] with the identical tallit."[4] Even in death, there is no ostentatious display for the rich. Every Jewish man is interred in simple

בָּרוּךְ אַתָּה יְיָ אֱלֹהֵינוּ מֶלֶךְ הָעוֹלָם אֲשֶׁר
קִדְּשָׁנוּ בְּמִצְוֹתָיו וְצִוָּנוּ לְהִתְעַטֵּף בַּצִּיצִית:

—Blessing recited when preparing to wrap oneself in *Tallit* white clothing and his own *tallit*. Indeed, the *tallit* may well have been the fine linen shroud or the "napkin" used in the interment of Jesus.

Before putting on the four-cornered garment, Jewish men for some nineteen centuries have recited the following benediction: "Blessed art thou, O Lord, our God, King of the universe, who has sanctified us by thy commandments, and has commanded us to wrap ourselves in the *tzitzit*." While it is believed that this benediction dates to the Tannaic period after the destruction of the Temple, it is possible that Jesus recited some form of it. Today, this same benediction is embroidered on the *atarah* (crown) of most prayer shawls so that a man may see the blessing as he recites it.

In modern times, the *tallit* is worn each day during the morning prayers (*Shacharit*), except on the Ninth of Av, when it is worn at the afternoon service, and on *Yom Kippur* (the Day of Atonement), when it is worn all day. The *tallit* is worn only during the day because the biblical commandment for its use specifies that the *tzitzit* must be *seen*.[5] In fact, the evening *Kol Nidrei* service on *Yom Kippur* begins before sunset, so that a Jew can wrap himself in his *tallit* while he can still see the *tzitziot*.[6]

Immediately after the recitation of the blessing, the *tallit* is put on, covering the head first. Then, the four corners are thrown over the left shoulder, a movement called *'atifat Yishme'elim* ("after the manner of the Ishmaelites, or Arabs").[7] After a short pause, the four corners are then allowed to fall back into their original position, two suspended on both sides of the worshipper.[8]

Strictly observant Jews pray with the *tallit* covering their head, believing that to be enfolded by the *tallit* is to be enveloped by the holiness of the commandments of the Torah, denoting symbolic subjection to the divine will.[9] It is also customary in the morning service to press the *tzitzit* to the eyes and to kiss them three times during the recital of the final section of the *Shema* which deals with the commandment of the *tzitzit*. As a praying mantle, the *tallit* expresses and conduces to a spirit of sublime devotion and consecrated meditation, inspiring in the heart a feeling of awe and reverence.[10] A token of the honor which the *tallit* is accorded is seen in the fact that whenever Torah scrolls are moved, they are generally covered in a *tallit* to protect them.

The *tallit* stands on solid biblical ground as a means of drawing the Jewish worshipper to attention so that he remembers the commandments of God and enters with *kavanah* (intensity and devotion) into his time of prayer for passionate, intimate relationship with God. Bible-believing Christians would do well to respect this tradition and the piety of the Jewish people who observe it in honor of God.

Objects of honor of one faith should not be exploited or abused by those of another. Christians should be careful to honor the importance of the *tallit* tradition for the Jewish community by not misusing or co-opting the *tallit* for their own purposes. Some use these and other accouterments of Judaism to make themselves appear Jewish in order to gain some advantage in "witnessing" to Jewish people, thinking that some-

how the end justifies the means. Such abuse and
deception is unethical and should not even be considered, much less practiced among Christians.
Others employ Jewish articles in an effort to in-
flate their own estimation of themselves as some-
how being "Jewish." Wearing Jewish liturgical
garments and displaying Jewish artifacts do not
make one Jewish any more than donning a robe
and a white wig makes one a British magistrate.

A growing number of Christians make such
use of traditionally Jewish things in an effort to
identify with the Jewish people and to demonstrate their understanding that their Christian faith
is inherently Jewish. While such a desire for Christians to identify with the Jewish people is com-
mendable, great care should be exercised not to
misuse or misrepresent Jewish traditions. The Jewish people are certainly not impressed when a *tallit*
is worn upside down, at the wrong time, or in
the wrong manner. Christians who rush off to
do Jewish things or to appear Jewish when they
obviously know nothing of the subject are at best
boorish and inconsiderate and at worst sacrile-
gious. We should remember that sensitivity is the
Golden Rule in action.

Great lessons about the Jewishness of Jesus
and the apostles can be learned from the articles
which they most certainly used in their own worship of God. Every material article–like every spiritual exercise–which was patterned and modeled
in the Hebrew Scriptures can be found in some
way to point to the Messiah. This is both Jesus'
and Paul's evaluation of the fundamental purpose
of the Torah.[11] Truths that are profoundly en-

hancing to Christian faith are readily discernible in Judaism and Jewish practices. Metaphors and allegories can be legitimately drawn from these sources in the same manner in which the New Testament writers did; however, care should be exercised when doing so to ensure that they are properly set in the context of the grammar and historico-cultural setting in which they were employed by the earliest church.

While Christians can certainly learn rich lessons about their Jewish Lord from the *tallit* tradition, they are not required to wear one when they pray. Indeed, the fulfillment of the command establishing *tzitzit* as a means of remembrance of God's commandments should be manifest in a fully biblical lifestyle of walking in the Holy Spirit and letting the light of God's Messiah shine through one's good works of obedience to God's Word. Christian believers who fully experience the living Christ are not merely enshrouded in the Torah, they are imbued with the living Torah through the indwelling lawgiver, the Holy Spirit.

It is unlikely that pious, Torah-observant Jews would begrudge Christians the legitimate, respectful use of any Jewish artifact that would draw a believer closer to God and his Word in pure, sincere devotion. If wearing a prayer shawl during times of prayer helps one to focus on and interact with the Divine, one could profit from such. If one is convicted by the Holy Spirit (not by one's own soulish impulses) that he should practice Jewish things, such an exercise is legitimate and is birthed in freedom, not in legalism. They can certainly enhance various practices in Christian churches that are designed to focus the worshipper's attention on God and his service. If ministers wish to use a *tallit* as a vestment or if churches wish to use it as a decoration in their sanctuaries at significant times to affirm their identity with the Jewish people, such use is appropriate. Objects like the *shofar*, the *menorah*, the *chanukiah*, the *tallit*, the *mezuzah*, the *matzah*, the *kiddush* cup, the Torah scroll, and others can add depth and richness to the Christian worship experience when they are identified with the living Christ.

A classic example of this depth that is added to the Christian experience by understanding the Hebraic matrix from which Christianity emerged is the subject of this book, the *tallit* tradition of biblical, Second Temple, and Rabbinic Judaism. As we have seen, this tradition impacted the lives of prophets, kings, and ancestors of the Messiah in the Hebrew Scriptures and of Jesus, his disciples, and the people to whom they ministered in the New Covenant era. Without an understanding of this rich biblical tradition from the Judaic heritage of Christian faith, we have an incomplete view of what actually happened in Jesus' ministry. We are left to draw our own conclusions based on our cultures and traditions. With this background of the circumstances that were the context of events in the Gospels, we share a richness that expands our understanding and invigorates our faith. And, this is but one small element in the vast treasure house of riches that awaits those who search diligently to discover the Hebraic truths that often lie just beneath the surface of our Bible translations. Understanding the Hebrew foundations of our Christian faith is, indeed, a golden key that unlocks the treasures of Holy Scripture for those who passionately pursue the truths of God's living, infinite, immutable Word.

[1] Theodor Reik. *Pagan Rites in Judaism* (New York, Simon & Schuster, 1944), pp. 142-144.
[2] Martin Samuel Cohen. "The Tallit," *Conservative Judaism* 44 (Spring, 1992), p. 4.
[3] Rudolph Brasch, p. 240.
[4] Rudolph Brasch, p. 240.
[5] Alfred J. Kolatch, p. 101.
[6] Rudolph Brasch, pp. 238-239.
[7] Alfred J. Kolatch, p. 103.
[8] *Encyclopaedia Judaica* - CD-ROM Edition (Jerusalem: Judaica Multimedia, Ltd.).
[9] *Encyclopaedia Judaica*.
[10] Rudolph Brasch, p. 240.
[11] John 5:39; Colossians 2:17.

Want To Know More?

If you have enjoyed *Touching the Hem*'s introduction to the Jewish prayer shawl in the ministry of Jesus, you will be powerfully impacted by Dr. Garr's book, *The Hem of His Garment: Touching the Power in God's Word*, a thorough, scholarly study of the prayer shawl tradition that discusses numerous biblical themes that are impacted by a clear understanding of the clothing that the Jewish people wore. You will simply be amazed at the richness of the Christian heritage in this simple biblical Jewish practice.

Acquire these

LIVING EMBLEMS

both for your own personal use and for teaching.

Prayer Shawls and other Jewish emblems, either specifically commanded in Holy Scripture or designed by the Jewish people to fulfill divine instructions, are available from

Restoration Foundation
P. O. Box 421218
Atlanta, GA 30342, U.S.A.
www.RestorationFoundation.org

For a complete catalog of these and other items of Judaica call

Holy Land Gifts
(1-800-564-4659)

Other Books by Dr. Garr

The Hem of His Garment: Touching the Power in God's Word.

God's Lamp: Man's Light: Mysteries of the Menorah.

Living Emblems: Ancient Symbols of Faith

Our Lost Legacy: Christianity's Hebrew Heritage

Bless You: The Power of the Biblical Blessing

The Book of Blessings: Biblical Blessings for Every Occasion

Feminine & Free! Restoring God's Design for Women

The Church Dynamic: Hebraic Foundations for Christian Community

Jesus: When God Became Human

Divine Appointments: Meeting with God

Think Not! Boast Not! Christianity's Sin against the Jews

Christian Fruit, Jewish Root: Restoring the Health of the Branches

Restoration Foundation

Understanding the Jewish roots of our faith is a golden key that unlocks the treasures of Holy Scripture and enables us to enrich our Christian lives. This fundamental concept is the focus of Restoration Foundation, an international, transdenominational, multi-cultural, and interracial educational and publishing resource to the body of Christ.

Restoration Foundation features a network of scholars, church leaders, and laypersons who share the vision for restoring to the church the Hebrew foundations of our Christian faith and returning the church to a biblical relationship of love and support for the international Jewish community and the nation of Israel.

We are pleased to make available to all denominations and fellowships the teaching of the gifted scholars and Christian leaders in our network. Conferences, seminars, and other instructional forums are available on a wide range of topics that can be tailored to each individual setting. We also teach these concepts throughout the world with our International Institutes.

We publish *Restore!* magazine, a high-quality journal featuring theological balance and scholarly documentation which helps Christians recover their Hebrew heritage while strengthening their faith in Jesus.

Restoration Foundation also publishes and distributes Golden Key Books in order to disseminate teaching about Christianity's Judaic foundations.

The ministry of Restoration Foundation is made possible by our many partners around the world who share in our Golden Key Partnership program. If you would like to join us, you will have the satisfaction of knowing that you are a partner in an organization that is making a difference in the world by restoring Christians to their biblical Hebrew heritage, by eradicating Judaeophobia and anti-Semitism, by supporting Israel and the international Jewish community, and by encouraging collaborative efforts among those who share this vision.

For information about Restoration Foundation, *Restore!* magazine, Golden Key Books, and Golden Key Partnerships, contact us at the address below.

Restoration Foundation
P. O. Box 421218
Atlanta, Georgia 30342, U.S.A.
www.RestorationFoundation.org

Hebraic Heritage Christian Center

Hebraic Heritage Christian Center is an institution of higher education that is dedicated to the vision of restoring a Hebraic model for Christian education. A consortium of scholars, spiritual leaders, and business persons, the Center features a continually developing curriculum in which each course of study is firmly anchored in the Hebrew foundations of the Christian faith.

The Hebraic Heritage Christian Center vision combines both the ancient and the most modern in an educational program that conveys knowledge, understanding, and wisdom to a world-wide student population. The Center seeks to restore the foundations of original Christianity in order to equip its students with historically accurate, theologically sound understanding of the biblical faith that Jesus and the apostles instituted and practiced. At the same time the Center endeavors to implement the finest in innovative, cutting-edge technology in a distance-learning program that delivers its user-friendly courses by the Internet.

Among the wide range of services and products that Hebraic Heritage Christian Center offers are the publications of Hebraic Heritage Press. These are delivered both in traditional print media as well as in electronic media to serve both the Center's student population and the general public with inspiring and challenging materials that have been developed by the Center's team of scholars.

Those who are interested in sharing in the development of Hebraic Heritage Christian Center and its commitment to restoring the Jewish roots of the Christian faith are invited to join the Founders' Club, people who support this team of scholars and leaders by becoming co-founders of this institution. Many opportunities for endowments are also available to those who wish to create a lasting memorial to the cause of Christian renewal and Christian-Jewish rapprochement.

Get Your Free Copy of

**The Magazine That's Restoring the Biblically Hebraic
Heritage to Christian Believers Around the World**

Restore! is the exciting new journal that's. . .

✡ *helping Christians around the world to restore the Jewish roots of their faith in Jesus Christ.*

✡ *fighting against Judaeophobia, anti-Judaism, and anti-Semitism in the Christian church.*

✡ *encouraging Christians to support the international Jewish community and the nation of Israel.*

✡ *promoting unity (cohesiveness in the midst of diversity) within the universal body of Christ*

HERE'S WHAT SOME OF OUR READERS ARE SAYING ABOUT *Restore!*

"I consider *Restore!* to be the best magazine on the restoration of Jewish roots because of its quality of presentation of the various topics, its scholarly articles, and most important, the strengthening of our faith that results the articles."—Michael Katritsis, Athens, Greece.

"*Restore!* is the best magazine I have ever read, the only one which I have read cover to cover."—Colyn King, Levin, New Zealand.

"*Restore!* is an inspiration both in its quality and the profundity of its contents."—Jorge Robles Olarte, Medellin, Columbia.

> **Discover for yourself the Jewish roots of your faith as you read the informative, provocative material in the pages of *Restore!***

✂ -
❑ Please send me a free sample copy of *Restore!*
❑ Please enter my subscription to *Restore!* $25/yr. ($35 outside U.S.)
❑ Please bill my ❑Visa ❑American Express ❑Discover ❑MasterCard
#_____Exp._____
Name_____
Address_____
City_____State_____Code_____Nation_____

Restoration Foundation
P. O. Box 421218, Atlanta, GA 30342 E-Mail: info@restorationfoundation.org

Restore!

Restoration Foundation

P. O. Box 421218
Atlanta, GA 30342